FINDING THE
ANSWER

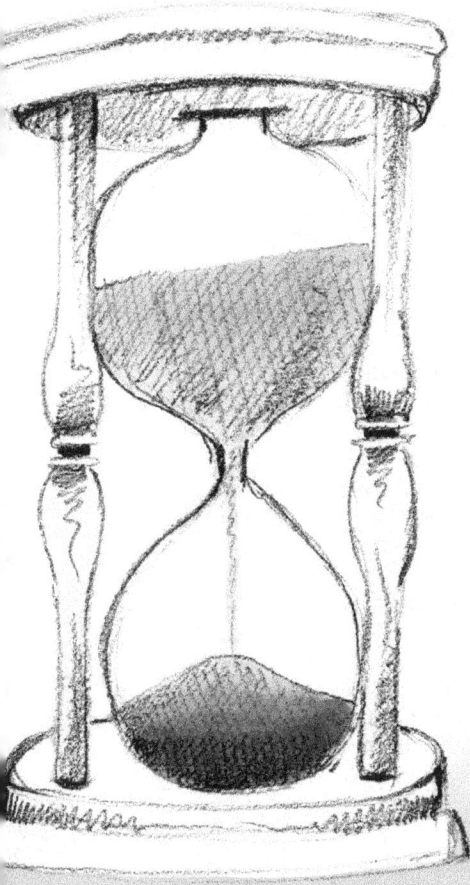

TO OVERCOME THE CHALLENGES OF LIFE, HAVE PEACE, AND SECURE MY FUTURE

JOHN CALE

Selah Press
PUBLISHING
NASHVILLE, TENNESSEE

DEDICATION

"Please stop talking"..."Be quiet"...These were the words I heard come from my mother, Stella Pearl Cale (Sanchez), throughout my childhood. I admit I had a problem with being quiet and sitting still. Stella was the mother of six children who were all older—the closest one to me was 11 years older than me. Mom had faced a lot before I came around. But, she told me that I was another level of child raising.

I share this story because I want to dedicate this book to my mom, Stella. She loved people and truly lived a life of letting God use her to love and reach out to others around her. She was a pray-er and many people's lives and eternities were impacted by her prayers.

Just as I heard comments about my behavior through my childhood, I also started hearing, "Son, you need to pray more and let God help you"...Every time I saw her, I heard these words. She prayed for all her children, including me. Without her reminders and ongoing prayers, I seriously don't think I would have lived up to this point. Thank you, Mom, for giving of yourself and praying for me.

My hope is that this book will be an extension of your life to help new generations of people to know Him. I love you Mom.

CONTENTS

Still Searching...

REALIZE—SOMETHING IS MISSING

ANSWERS...You and I have been searching for them for all our lives...and we still are! The fact that you picked up this little book and are reading it proves that you are still looking for answers.

Let's start with an important fact about this book...
The purpose of this 104-page read **IS NOT** to tell you how and what to do to find answers...**IT IS ABOUT** having a discussion around thoughts and questions that will present you with **an opportunity to find the answers and prove them on your own.**

So, what do we mean by answers, anyway? The Oxford Dictionary says an answer is: "A thing said, written, or done to deal with or as a reaction to a question, statement, or situation."[1]

Simply put, answers are the responses to questions raised about situations we are dealing with.

To see a video about this topic from John Cale, open the camera on your phone, hold your phone over the QR code above, and click open on your browser.

FINDING THE ANSWER

The challenges we are dealing with...Do these few words raise your anxiety or stress level? And doesn't the idea of having answers to deal with these challenges bring you a sense of calm?

What are the life situations that you are dealing with right now?

What are the top questions that you need answers to?

Everyone has different issues, but the one common theme for all of us is that **the questions we face and the answers we desire are real, needed, and pressing.**

FINDING THE ANSWER

The result of not having these answers is ultimately unwanted STRESS. Stress affects our mood, sleep, job performance, and our health. Stress impacts both the person we are on the inside, as well as how people see us on the outside. Both our outward reflections and the true pictures of who we are become distorted with stress. Something seems off and missing.

This daily stress increases as we search for answers with information coming at us from all angles. With the world at our fingertips via our mobile devices, tablets, laptops, and "the Cloud," don't you find it strange that we are still seeking—and actually have even more of an insatiable need for—information? Texts, IMs, Tweets, Instagram, and Facebook lives, posts, reels, and stories, Snapchats, Tiktoks, emails, calls, podcasts, Ted Talks, and blogs are all stimulating our minds and have us wound up and thinking constantly.

STILL, with all of these media options, we continue to have questions and we are still in search of answers...

We want answers—not just to day-to-day, minor issues—**but to larger questions**, like: *Why is my life not what I thought it would be when I was younger? Why can't I find the love of my life? Why did I lose my job when I am an honest and hard worker? Why was my life stricken with a critical illness? Why is there so much anger and hate in the world? Why did my spouse cheat on me? Why does this addiction and substance abuse continue to plague my life day after day when I don't want it in my life? What happened to the American Dream of college followed by a great and successful career for life? Why was my loved one taken so soon?*

And the list goes on and on...

What is life all about anyway? Do I live here for maybe 90 years and then leave everything I accumulated to someone else...and then what? That sure doesn't seem encouraging or make a lot of sense...

I think, if we admit it, we find ourselves thinking...*Is this really it? What am I here for? What's next?* Our days are filled with highs and lows, good and bad, the planned and unexpected, the new and the reminder of the old, and yet, it seems we always circle back to these questions that leave us asking, wandering, and being uneasy.

These questions drive feelings that come at times when our minds are triggered by a place or circumstance—or even when things are quiet. Although the circumstances or triggers may be temporary, **the intensity of the questions grow as time moves on**...

FINDING THE ANSWER

Often times, these questions are accompanied with feelings of emptiness, loneliness, and thoughts that something or someone is missing from our lives. We become convinced that whatever or whoever is missing will really make us fulfilled, and ultimately, complete.

Don't you find it amazing that in the midst of being surrounded daily by people at work, with our families, or just going through our normal daily tasks, that we can still feel alone?

Maybe the uncertain times we live in drive us to this lonely and isolated place of reflection to get answers. The daily tragedies and unfathomable violence that we see all around us—both near and far—can cause us to question and intensify our search for answers.

The timing of when the best time to find the answers we are seeking is important to consider.

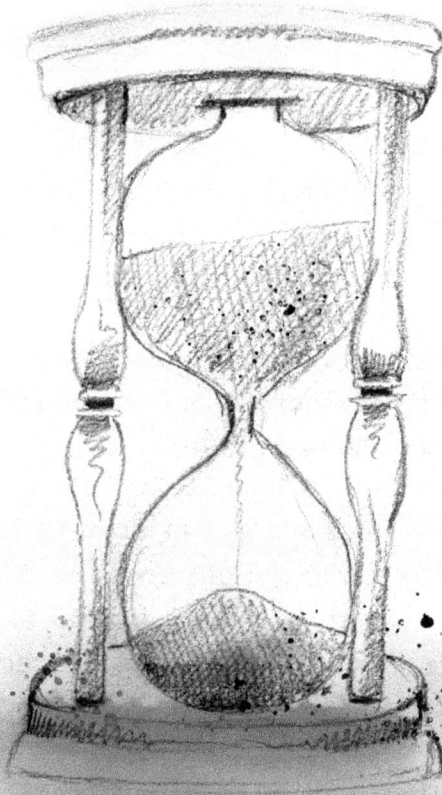

Maybe, right now, while there is no major "drama" or "trauma" that has your world rocked sideways, is a perfect time to seek answers.

Now—when you can think straight and are not significantly distracted—is a perfect time for you to find and prove for yourself not just answers, but The Answer that can change your life.

FINDING THE ANSWER

Seriously...What would happen if you found something that changed you and finally filled the void you have been searching to fill all your life? What would also happen, if you, **and only you**, could tell your friends and family your personal story about the experience you had? If that scenario happened, wouldn't that be amazing?

Stick with me. Let me help you consider some factors that will lead you closer to The Answer you seek. These factors will help provide clarity about how the ins and outs of life have brought you to where you are right now.

FINDING THE ANSWER

CONSIDER—AN HONEST REFLECTION

We are going to pause and take a few minutes to reflect here...Why? I am going to ask you to commit to be genuinely honest with yourself as you continue to read the following pages. Please take a really hard look at who you are and **how you got here**...this step is vitally important to finding The Answer you are seeking.

You see, our lives are each unique. Although we all face similar types of tasks and activities day after day as we live on this spinning ball called Planet Earth, the lens we each look through portrays a personalized view. **Our views are tied directly to the things, people, places, experiences, answers, advice, and so on, that have paved our lifelong journeys.**

To see a video about this topic from John Cale, open the camera on your phone, hold your phone over the QR code above, and click open on your browser.

"Our childhood is crucial
to who we are today."
— John Cale

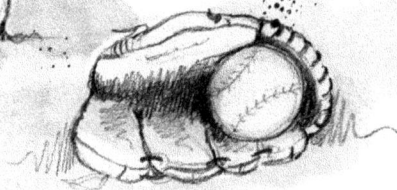

Think about your views and your life journey so far...Where did you go to get your answers in life as you were growing up?...Parents? Teachers? Media? Friends? Church? Our childhood is crucial to who we are today. How do I know?...Let's reflect on some real-life personal situations you may have experienced.

FINDING THE ANSWER

Think right now about any experiences you may have had as a child when you were made fun of, embarrassed, shamed, or abused. These experiences pop up to the front of your mind immediately... You can probably even see the scene, the people, the room and even the clothes you may have had on just like it was yesterday. The same phenomenon is true for the good times—you remember the praise, accolades, success, and the trophies you attained.

THE POINT IS...OUR CHILDHOOD SETS THE FOUNDATION AND COLOR AROUND HOW WE FUNCTION AND SEE LIFE NOW.

FINDING THE ANSWER

So, as we have grown up over the years, we have searched for answers to the many questions in our lives...Sometimes, you may have felt you had found behavioral "answers" for various life situations.

For example, you may have learned that if you perform well, you may have gotten praised and in turn felt good about yourself for a time.

Or, if you got bullied, you could have either run away or given someone what they wanted so you could get out of a harmful situation.

These behavioral "answers" or others like them must have served you fairly well because you made it to this point—right?

Yet, many life situations are still left without answers, and in many cases, any answers we thought we had found just led to more and more questions that we have never thought of before.

"Holding on is believing that there's only a past; letting go is knowing that there's a future."
— Daphne Rose Kingma

Perhaps we have gotten some answers along the way, and perhaps they have lessened some of our uneasiness—for a time. But as we experience even greater challenges, we wonder about the answers' validity. **For us to accept an answer, we have to trust**. We have to feel we can trust how we get answers and believe **that they are true and accurate**. The challenge we all face in today's world is **"Trust."**

FINDING THE ANSWER

I believe we would admit that we have all traveled the road to trust something or someone...Whether it be a relationship, a substance or addiction, success, or something else...

I think we could acknowledge that we tend to run from thing to thing and engage in it, hoping that it will be the answer to questions we have. We are hoping "the new thing" addresses the emptiness that continues to remain day in and day out. **What are the things you are often running after in your life?**

What follows on the next few pages are a few common things we are all looking for.

You have the power to say, "This is not how my story will end."

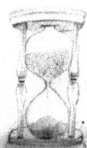

The Career/Success—Nothing like the new job, right? New people and the challenge of a whole new setting for our lives...Oh, and in many cases, a promotion, and a big fat raise, too. Everything is great at the beginning...remember? Then, over time, the excitement fades. We find the new problems, and the new challenge becomes the same old routine—day after day. People come and go, and that feeling that **something is missing** creeps up again, driving us to start searching for something more, fresh, and new.

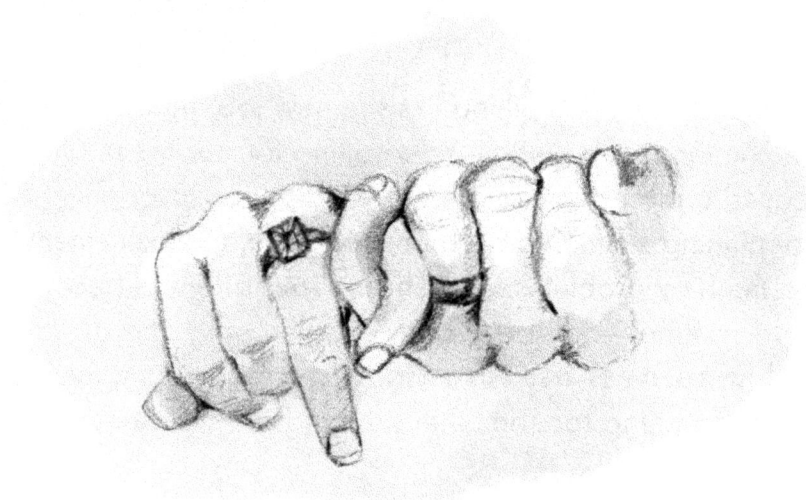

The Soul Mate—Yes..."THE ONE." Perfect in every way...looks... build...background...personality. We search so hard to find **"the one"** who will make us feel complete so that we can share the rest of our lives with someone. Maybe you have found him or her... maybe you are still searching. Even if you have found "the one" who is everything you were searching for, over time, things begin to change. The looks, the personality, your circumstances move into a different place, and again, there is this feeling: *Is there something more or something better?*

Even the greatest relationships have hard times, but in all reality, the divorce rates prove it with one of every two marriages failing. The dream changes and folks are left searching again...the dream fades.

"Our focus is shifted by a sound,
a smell, person or other things."

The Shiny—Here is a word you may remember from the movie *Up*, or if you didn't see that movie, you have at least heard..."squirrel." It is a reference to our propensity to be distracted easily by something that gets our attention...Focus is shifted by a sound, a smell, a person, or something else. We are drawn to the "new" and "shiny" things in life. What gets your attention? Is it the awesome sleek and perfect colored new car, the fashion statement outfit and accompanied accessories, the newest and top furnished home in the best neighborhood, or the vacation home in the dream setting? Many more items could be added to this list.

I'm sure you have found, as I have, that NOTHING STAYS NEW. The new car loses that new car smell, the paint gets scratched, and the body gets the famous door dings—no matter how far we try to park away from others. Our clothes wear and fade, and the house gets damaged, stained, and becomes weathered over time. Back to the same familiar situation once again...We are not satisfied, and we have a gnawing desire for something more...

The Approval/Acceptance Factor—One thing that all of us living on this planet want is to feel accepted for who we are.

We long to have the approval of our friends, family, peers, co-workers, etc. We want to feel that people value the person we are and what we have to offer. We all have unique skills, talents, and abilities, and typically, we find a sense of worth and value around these things and how well we do them.

There has to be something more...

So, as you think through the questions you may have faced, you will likely see that there is a common theme...Things change, we find ourselves still searching for something new, and that feeling of ***there has to be something more*** continues to plague us. **We continue our search for answers.**

Think with me for a minute to prove the point that we will always be searching for more...How can movie stars, singers, and successful business professionals who have it all still have this feeling of emptiness? They have money, cars, homes, relationships, fame, drugs, fortune, family, and the promise of a storybook future, yet they search and run hard after more. In the end, many of these seemingly successful people take their own lives or overdose DESPITE HAVING EVERYTHING. They cannot fill the emptiness and loneliness they feel. This choice is so sad and brings such pain and anguish to those who love these people. Think for a moment of the celebrities you know who this has happened to.

Why?

Perhaps they became hopeless when they couldn't find an answer, or maybe they gave up on life after nothing they obtained satisfied them. Perhaps they were looking in an elusive place for a mysterious person or to fleeting fame and fortune for fulfillment. In reality, we are created as spiritual beings who need a spiritual answer. There is part of us that nothing of the physical realm can ever really fill. No matter how hard we try and search, nothing material or no human person can fill that empty gnawing feeling way down inside of each of us that never is satisfied.

Would you consider looking at a different approach? A fresh way of thinking—that you may have never considered—could be The Answer.

A key word paves the pathway to The Answer...

Relationship.

Understanding the reality and power of this word can change the rest of your life.

APPLY—A PERSONAL, PRIVATE APPROACH

Relationship is defined as... "The way in which two or more concepts, objects, or peoples are connected...or the state of being connected."[2] We simply **"put ourselves out there"** to believe in someone or something. Our emotions, heart, and being are all involved. We find ourselves at a crossroads where we have to decide, based on the information we have—whether a little or a lot—to step out and TAKE A CHANCE TO TRUST.

How many times have you "trusted" someone and been let down, hurt, or devastated? How and why does this happen to us—sometimes over and over again? **Is it possible that we really don't understand relationships?** Maybe you were not raised in a home where you saw and experienced the pattern of healthy relationships. Perhaps you have never realized the power and need to really understand that healthy relationships can make or ruin your life.

To see a video about this topic from John Cale, open the camera on your phone, hold your phone over the QR code above, and click open on your browser.

A key truth is that **relationships are based on trust**. Your relationships with your friends, significant other, employer, family members, and even your furry friend(s) revolve around trust. Trust is built over a period of time—day after day. Repeated actions that follow what you agreed upon prove to you that, whatever the relationship you are engaged in, you can continue to feel more comfortable with the relationship. This ease strengthens your trust and allows you to become more vulnerable.

I want to ask you to consider this question...Where did you get your example or pattern for a relationship?

When you think about this question, is there a picture or song that pops up when you think of the word relationship? Is it associated with a good or bad feeling?

I think you would agree with me that not many (if any) of us ever had someone sit us down and open a big book on relationships. We weren't taught what healthy relationships are, how to have a successful one, the power they have, or how they will impact us for the rest of our lives. Most of us went from childhood to adulthood living life and formed an internal opinion based on the examples we saw around us.

$$=$$

Trust / ~~Trust~~

Maybe your model for relationships was your parents. Good or bad—your mother, father, or a guardian impacted how you see relationships now as an adult. Maybe it was a combination of your friends' parents, shows you watched on TV, the music you listened to and the stories they told, some books or literature you read, or some other source. You see, our backgrounds determine whether we can trust quickly or if we have a hard time ever trusting.

When our trust is violated, we are devastated...Our best friend turns on us out of nowhere. We thought everything we believed in would be lasting...and it is not.

We feel lied to and we become very angry.

Ultimately our anger is a "cover emotion" for the hurt we don't want anyone to know we are feeling deep inside... Take a minute...Be honest with yourself and look at your life. Underneath your times of anger, in most cases, it is likely that you felt hurt or disappointment.

So, let's get straight to some different thoughts that will point you to a new approach.

"A good friend knows all your stories...a best friend helped you write them"...

Who do you currently have a strong relationship with? Is it with your best friend? Maybe you would rather think of someone in your past who was this individual. Why are or were they so close to you? Why do you trust them so much? My guess is that you've spent a lot of time with them—perhaps you had fun times in social settings, maybe you experienced some painful downs of life, or perhaps you shared times of celebration and key milestones in your journey.

These people know you well. They know your favorite food, your preferred clothing style, the way you react, your likes and dislikes, and they even know your daily choices and routine.

THIS IS ALL POSSIBLE **BECAUSE YOU SPENT CONSISTENT TIME WITH THEM AND ACTUALLY KNOW THEM PERSONALLY...**YOU HAVE PROVED THAT THEY ARE TRUSTWORTHY, AND YOU KNOW IT.

Please take a moment to go through this story with me.

Imagine your best friend coming to you and telling you that they had just run into someone that spent five minutes telling him or her what an idiot you are…This someone had said that you are selfish, egotistical, and are a liar who can't be trusted. (If this has happened to you in real life, please, stay with me here.) You can't believe what you are hearing, right? You share with your friend that this individual they met has only ever talked to you once for less than five minutes… "They don't even know me," you say. Your mind is blown because you can't imagine why someone would do this.

You mind goes round and round, trying to understand…You ask yourself questions, like: *Are they confusing me with someone else? Has someone else told them something about me that is not true? Maybe they are jealous of me? Maybe they just didn't like a social post I made?*

At the core of this difficulty, you keep thinking some combination of… *They don't have any idea who I really am, they don't know what I am like, or they think I am someone I am not.*

You see, the only way to know someone, or to straighten out any misperceptions is to come to the source…the person…and have a relationship with that person.

OK my friend, please stay with me here...I am going to ask you to consider something you may not have ever thought of before...

Have you ever considered that **this story—the one we just walked through happens with God every day?**

Perhaps you would be willing to entertain this possibility that this story could apply to God—and to your perception of Him.

Start by asking yourself a few questions: *Who do you think He is? Why do you think of Him this way? Have you believed things you have heard others say about Him, things you have read or seen? Have you been hurt or disappointed by the church? Were you taught RULES WITH NO RELATIONSHIP?* We could ask more questions, but you get the idea.

Just as in the story we walked through—the one that you felt so upset, confused, and angry about, because this person had no idea who you were...**God feels this way every day because of being misunderstood by tens of millions of people.**

"You can't be perfect enough, give enough, go to church enough, be nice enough to meet God...you meet him just the way you are."

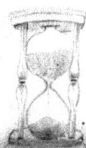

You see, despite all that you have seen and heard up to this point about God or religion, the crux of the matter is so simple...God wants you to come to Him to see who He is. **He loves you as you are**, and He wants to start a relationship with you today.

You see, you don't have to be perfect to meet Him. He wants to meet you just as you are...*Did you catch that?* Right where you are...you don't need to change anything.

ASK YOURSELF THIS QUESTION...*Have you ever gone directly to God yourself—just you—and asked Him to show you if He is real?*

Just as we outlined how going to the actual source personally is the only way to prove who someone is and develop a relationship**, the same approach is what we need to do to meet this awesome God.**

OK...so you may be thinking, ***This is it—a relationship with God? All this reading and this is The Answer?***

Yes, my friend...Before you underestimate a relationship with God, have you really ever had one?...

Have you put aside what everyone else says, what you've read, what you have seen, what you think and just simply ask him yourself to form a relationship with you?

This is the crossroads where you can choose to get your Answer.

I wrote this book because this is the most organic and real way for you to prove His reality personally without any other influence but **YOU AND HIM.**

It is not by chance you have picked this book up or it was given to you...NOW IS YOUR CHANCE TO SEE WHO HE IS AND REALIZE HIS DESIRE TO KNOW YOU.

I have made it very simple and private for you.

You are now at a decision point with two choices...

1. Do Nothing... Put the book away and let this experience pass you by with the potential life changing impacts that could be yours... You can continue to search for an answer and remain in the same mode of life you were in before you invested the time to search for The Answer.

2. Prove it for yourself... Choose one of the two options outlined on page 65 that best fits where you are in life right now. You, and you alone, once and for all, can get your Answer. Today could be the beginning of a new pathway that you have never traveled on before which could result in a happier, less stressful, and more fulfilled life in which the vicious cycle of "there must be something more" could come to an end.

It is time for you to choose...Choose wisely...Take a chance...

EXPERIENCE—The Authenticity of THE ANSWER

Option 1—"The Challenge"

If you have developed a deeper curiosity and an unusual feeling within that you can't really explain as you've read up to this point in the book, "The Challenge" is for you. "The Challenge" section provides you with a 25-day self-investigation to allow you to be honest and open your mind to seek and receive The Answer. This investigation will equip you to address daily the ongoing feelings of emptiness and to search for something more. Day by day as you journey through "The Challenge," you may begin to see things differently, sense new things altogether, or both. Go to page 67 to start "The Challenge."

Option 2—"Meeting Him"

If, as you have read this book up to this point, you have had various scenes or "self-videos" playing in your head of life situations that seem pertinent, choosing the "Meeting Him" section could be your next step.

If you have a sense that something needs to change right now, and you feel a strong internal "nudge" compelling you, this option is your next step. "Meeting Him" is a section that empowers you to begin a relationship with God based on where your life circumstances are TODAY. Begin the section on page 99 honestly and with openness.

To see a video about this topic from John Cale, open the camera on your phone, hold your phone over the QR code above, and click open on your browser.

OPTION 1—"THE CHALLENGE"

GETTING STARTED

1. Don't change anything about your life...
Just get started.

2. Don't change anything about your life...
Just get started...**This repetition is not a misprint...**Don't be tempted to fix or change
anything in your life now...Just start...JUST AS YOU
ARE with all you habits, hang-ups, attitudes, anger, disappointments, wealth or
poverty, and everything else...**Just be sincere each day.**

3. Find 20 minutes a day to do the challenge...A consistent time and place
alone where it is quiet is helpful.

4. Sign below to commit to yourself to finish this 25-day journey to finding
your "Answer."

_____ (Sign & Date)

5. Do your best to do "The Challenge" 25 days in a row. If you miss some days,
it's OK...Just be sure to finish the 25 days.

6. If at any time during your challenge, you have a desire and are feeling drawn
to start a relationship with God, to ask for forgiveness, or to pray, skip to the
section following "The Challenge" called "Meeting Him."

7. John encourages you to record your questions in the space provided on the upcoming pages. If you'd like to interact with John as you go through your journey, email john@findingtheasnwerbook.com with questions as you go through your journey.

To see a video about this topic from John Cale, open the camera on your phone, hold your phone over the QR code above, and click open on your browser.

PRAYER TO START CHALLENGE

Read or say the following prayer: "God, I ask that you give me the strength to complete this challenge. I ask you to bring your presence to help me take the daily steps to meet you for who you are. In Jesus' name I pray. Amen." Once you meet Him, your life will never be the same again...

DAILY "CHALLENGE" INSTRUCTIONS

1. A simple opening prayer is listed for each day to get you started...This prayer will help you get centered, and with the prayer, you are giving God permission to speak to you. He is not a dictator...He respects your choice and your will to make choices. You do, however, need to give him permission by inviting him to personally engage with you about your life.

2. Read the verses from the Gospel of Mark for that day. You can use your Bible or go online to biblegateway.com, click on read, and type in Mark followed by the chapter and verses, choose the NIV version, and read there for the day.

3. Spend a couple minutes thinking/meditating about what you read. You can also search online for more about the cultural or historical background, the locations/maps where the verses take place, the people involved, or other details about the passage that may intertest you.

4. End each day with the closing prayer. This prayer gives God permission to speak to you and to TEACH you more about what you just read. God's Spirit is "The Teacher"...He is the part of God who will apply what you read to your specific life situations and challenges to bring change in your life.

BASIC BIBLE BACKGROUND INFORMATION

1. Why read the book of Mark, and who was he?

    a. Mark is also known as John Mark. He traveled with Paul, who wrote a large portion of the New Testament. He also traveled with Peter and accompanied him in Rome when he was imprisoned. He would most likely have been a teenager during Jesus' ministry years. Jesus' mother Mary's house was a place where believers in Jesus were welcome.

    b. Mark begins with Jesus' baptism by John the Baptist and the beginning of Jesus' three-year ministry before his death and Resurrection. Mark's account is concise, and it covers the time Jesus spent on Earth and a portion of what he accomplished and established.

    c. If you would like to read about the events around the birth of Jesus, go to Luke, Chapters 1–3. These chapters detail the virgin birth of Jesus in Bethlehem, which we celebrate as Christmas today. Additional background prior to the beginning of Jesus' ministry, which is where the Gospel of Mark starts, is also available.

2. The Bible is God's message to mankind in writing. It has survived for thousands of years and sold billions and billions of copies. The things written in the Bible, including the people and places mentioned, are not only true and factual but also backed up over and over again by history and science.

BASIC BIBLE BACKGROUND INFORMATION
Continued

There are two major sections to the Bible: the Old Testament and the New Testament. The Old Testament records much of the history, including the creation of man, the break in relationship between man and God, and the background of why God would need to bring Jesus to Earth to restore our relationship with him. The New Testament covers the arrival of Jesus on Earth through his birth to a virgin (Mary), a portion of his 33-year life, and the spread of God 's (his Father) message of love and restoration, including Jesus' death, Resurrection, and return to his Father.

3. It is important to be aware that there are three parts to God, known as the Trinity. The three parts are God the Father, Jesus his Son, and the Holy Spirit, who is the teacher and messenger on behalf of God. Simply put, think of an egg which in itself is an egg but has three parts: the white, the yolk, and the shell...three in one.

SUPPORT MATERIALS/RESOURCES
TO ENHANCE YOUR JOURNEY:

1. Use your actual Bible or go to biblegateway.com to read online. As I mentioned in the instructions, I would recommend the NIV (New International Version). An alternative is the NLT (New Living Translation). These versions are easier to read and understand than the original King James Version, which you may have heard of. The documents and resources used in the King James Version of the Bible have not been changed in these versions...only the writing style is different.

2. If at some point you would like to buy a Bible, buy one online or search for "Christian Book stores near me," and you will find a list. A good Bible to consider is the NIV Life Application Bible. It has the commentary (an explanation) included on the bottom of the pages as you read the Bible verses.

3. If you would like help understanding the verses you read each day, you can go to the following website(s) or resources to access a commentary, which explains the background behind the verses you are reading. A commentary has expanded factual detail/research about the setting, people, and culture of the verses you are reading. Commentaries will follow in sequential order corresponding to the chapters and verses you are reading.

    a. Matthew Henry is a well-known and proven set of commentaries on the entire bible. The link below is for the book of Mark specifically. Go to biblestudytools.com, click on study, and then commentary.

    b. You can also search online for "Biblegateway Commentaries" and use another one if you like. You may have options to choose a version of the bible again like NIV, or New Living Translation.

    c. You can also go to *Christianity Today* magazine to find additional resources.

DAY 1

_____(Initial & Date)

OPENING PRAYER

"God, here I am...I ask, through the power of your Holy Spirit, that today, you show me who you are and that you love me...in Jesus' name I pray. Amen."

READING: Mark Chapter 1, Verses 1–28

THINK ABOUT:

- Jesus hung out with ordinary people.
- What kind of person was Jesus to have caused the fisherman to leave their livelihoods to follow him?
- Satan and demons are mentioned...Jesus had authority and power even over them.

_____

CLOSING PRAYER

"God, I give you permission, and I ask you to help me understand more about what I read today...in Jesus' name I pray. Amen."

MY THOUGHTS:_____

_____

_____

QUESTIONS (John also invites you to email questions to john@findingtheanswerbook.com.):

_____

_____

DAY 2

_____(Initial & Date)

OPENING PRAYER

"God, here I am...I ask, through the power of your Holy Spirit, that today, you to show me who you are and that you love me...in Jesus' name I pray. Amen."

READING: Mark Chapter 1, Verses 29–45

THINK ABOUT:

- Imagine being in the crowd and seeing Jesus heal the sick and diseased right in front of you.
- Even Jesus (God's Son) has to spend time away in relationship praying with his Father.
- What are your thoughts about healing?

_____

CLOSING PRAYER

"God, I give you permission, and I ask you to help me understand more about what I read today...in Jesus' name I pray. Amen."

MY THOUGHTS:_____

_____

_____

QUESTIONS (John also invites you to email questions to john@findingtheanswerbook.com.):

_____

_____

DAY 3

_____(Initial & Date)

PRAYER

"God, here I am...I ask, through the power of your Holy Spirit, that today, you show me who you are and that you love me...in Jesus' name, I pray. Amen."

READING: Mark Chapter 2, Verses 1–27

THINK ABOUT:

- Jesus sees our needs through life's clutter.
- Jesus is not in "a church;" he is at a dinner party building relationships with people.
- Rules and tradition have their place, but Jesus loves people first.

_____

CLOSING PRAYER

"God, I give you permission, and I ask you to help me understand more about what I read today, in Jesus' name I pray. Amen"

MY THOUGHTS:_____

_____

_____

QUESTIONS (John also invites you to email questions to john@findingtheanswerbook.com.):

_____

_____

_____

DAY 4

_____(Initial & Date)

PRAYER

"God, here I am...I ask, through the power of your Holy Spirit, that today, you show me who you are and that you love me...in Jesus' name I pray. Amen."

READING: Mark Chapter 3, Verses 1–34

THINK ABOUT:

- Loving people is a priority for Jesus.
- How would people who attend church/Christians accept Jesus if he appeared in society today?
- People were so judgmental that they missed the miracles.

_____

CLOSING PRAYER

"God, I give you permission, and I ask you to help me understand more about what I read today...in Jesus' name I pray. Amen."

MY THOUGHTS: _____

_____

_____

QUESTIONS (John also invites you to email questions to john@findingtheanswerbook.com.):

_____

_____

_____

DAY 5

_____(Initial & Date)

PRAYER

"God, here I am...I ask, through the power of your Holy Spirit, that today, you show me who you are and that you love me...in Jesus' name I pray. Amen."

READING: Mark Chapter 4, Verses 1–25

THINK ABOUT:

- What are the things I am distracted by?
- Jesus told stories and used illustrations to simplify his message, so people could understand it.
- How quick are we to judge people around us?

_____

CLOSING PRAYER

"God, I give you permission, and I ask you to help me understand more about what I read today...in Jesus' name I pray. Amen."

MY THOUGHTS:_____

_____

_____

QUESTIONS (John also invites you to email questions to john@findingtheanswerbook.com.):

_____

_____

_____

To see a video about this topic from John Cale, open the camera on your phone, hold your phone over the QR code above, and click open on your browser.

# DAY 6
_____(Initial & Date)

PRAYER

"God, here I am…I ask, through the power of your Holy Spirit, that today, you show me who you are and that you love me today…in Jesus' name I pray. Amen."

READING: Mark Chapter 4, Verses 26–41

THINK ABOUT:

- We all believe in something…to have "faith" is another level that unlocks the ability for God to change our lives.
- What does "faith" mean to you? What do you believe in?
- On a scale from 1 to 10, what number indicates your belief in what you read today and why?

_____

CLOSING PRAYER

"God, I give you permission, and I ask you to help me understand more about what I read today…in Jesus' name I pray. Amen."

MY THOUGHTS: _____

_____

_____

QUESTIONS (John also invites you to email questions to john@findingtheanswerbook.com.):

_____

_____

_____

DAY 7

_____(Initial & Date)

PRAYER

"God, here I am...I ask, through the power of your Holy Spirit, that today, you show me who you are and that you love me...in Jesus' name I pray. Amen."

READING: Mark Chapter 5, Verses 1–43

THINK ABOUT:

- Are there things in my life that have too much control over me?
- Isn't amazing that Jesus (God's Son) on purpose found people rejected by community and society to help?
- No one had to pay, be perfect, or do anything for Jesus to change their lives. All they had to do was to believe, ask, accept, and then follow him. The same offer applies to you.

_____

CLOSING PRAYER

"God, I give you permission, and I ask you to help me understand more about what I read today...in Jesus' name I pray. Amen."

MY THOUGHTS:_____

_____

_____

QUESTIONS (John also invites you to email questions to john@findingtheanswerbook.com.):

_____

_____

_____

DAY 8

_____(Initial & Date)

PRAYER

"God, here I am...I ask through the power of your Holy Spirit that today, you show me who you are and that you love me today...in Jesus' name, I pray. Amen."

READING: Mark Chapter 6, Verses 1–29

THINK ABOUT:

- Despite his miracles, many did not believe Jesus, and many hated him, which continues today. Why do you think people feel this way?
- Why is there a constant push to remove Jesus and God from our society at every turn?
- There is a spiritual battle happening around us daily between evil (satan) and good (God), who wants you to know his love, peace, and forgiveness. He wants you to join his family.

_____

CLOSING PRAYER

"God, I give you permission, and I ask you to help me understand more about what I read today...in Jesus' name I pray. Amen."

MY THOUGHTS:_____

_____

_____

QUESTIONS (John also invites you to email questions to john@findingtheanswerbook.com.):

_____

_____

_____

DAY 9

_____ (Initial & Date)

PRAYER

"God, here I am...I ask through the power of your Holy Spirit, that today, you show me who you are and that you love me...in Jesus' name I pray...Amen."

READING: Mark Chapter 6, Verses 30–56

THINK ABOUT:

- Because Jesus was God (The Creator) in the body of a man, his miracles here on Earth defy nature as we know it.
- Amazingly, 5,000 men and possibly 15,000 people (including wives and children) followed Jesus to a remote place to hear him. He fed them all in a miraculous display.
- Verses 51 and 52 allude to how "blown" the disciples minds were at the feeding of loaves and fish. Then Jesus walked on water. How would be feeling if you were in their shoes?

_____

CLOSING PRAYER

"God, I give you permission, and I ask you to help me understand more about what I read today...in Jesus' name I pray. Amen."

MY THOUGHTS:_____

_____

_____

QUESTIONS (John also invites you to email questions to john@findingtheanswerbook.com.):

_____

_____

_____

DAY 10

_____(Initial & Date)

PRAYER

"God, here I am...I ask, through the power of your Holy Spirit, that today, you show me who you are and that you love me...in Jesus' name I pray...Amen."

READING: Mark Chapter 7, Verses 1–37

THIINK ABOUT:

- Do you believe that outward actions are driven by what is within our hearts and being?
- What things are a part of your life that you wish you could change? Have you tried and been unsuccessful?
- Doesn't it seem that demons want to "attach" themselves to people throughout the events in the Bible? Notice Jesus' power is so strong that he healed them without being there in person.

_____

CLOSING PRAYER

"God, I give you permission and I ask you to help me understand more about what I read today...in Jesus' name I pray. Amen."

MY THOUGHTS:_____

_____

_____

QUESTIONS (John also invites you to email questions to john@findingtheanswerbook.com.):

_____

_____

_____

DAY 11

_____(Initial & Date)

PRAYER

"God, here I am...I ask, through the power of your Holy Spirit, that today, you show me who you are and that you love me...in Jesus' name I pray. Amen."

READING: Mark Chapter 8, Verses 1–38

THINK ABOUT:

- What did it take or what will it take for you to believe that Jesus is real? What is it that you think will prove it for you?
- What are your guidelines that determine what "genuine" is versus what "false" is when it comes to God?
- Can you imagine daily being in Jesus' shoes? He knew he was going to willingly die on a cross, and yet, he could have stopped it, but chose not to.

_____

CLOSING PRAYER

"God, I give you permission, and I ask you to help me understand more about what I read today...in Jesus' name I pray. Amen."

MY THOUGHTS:_____

_____

_____

QUESTIONS (John also invites you to email questions to john@findingtheanswerbook.com.):

_____

_____

_____

DAY 12

_____(Initial & Date)

PRAYER

"God, here I am...I ask, through the power of your Holy Spirit that today, you show me who you are and that you love me...in Jesus' name I pray. Amen."

READING: Mark Chapter 9, Verses 1–50

THINK ABOUT:

- Three normal men experienced Jesus' supernatural encounter with his Father. Relationship is shown as we know it.
- Do you wander at times why is there so much division over God? Our world judges based on "status," but God loves us all the same. With God, there is no special treatment or favors.
- What are some of the greatest temptations you are facing? How are you dealing with them?

_____

CLOSING PRAYER

"God, I give you permission, and I ask you to help me understand more about what I read today...in Jesus' name I pray. Amen."

MY THOUGHTS:_____

_____

_____

QUESTIONS (John also invites you to email questions to john@findingtheanswerbook.com.):

_____

_____

_____

DAY 13

_____(Initial & Date)

PRAYER

"God, here I am...I ask, through the power of Your Holy Spirit, that today, you show me who you are and that you love me...in Jesus' name I pray. Amen."

READING: Mark Chapter 10, Verses 1–31

THINK ABOUT:

- Think about how trusting and simple the faith of a little child is...Jesus says in verse 14 that God's Kingdom belongs to those who accept it simply.
- Is it possible that the blind beggar in verse 47 reveals a secret that if we cry out for help, Jesus will meet us? No matter who we are?
- We all would love to be rich...But, could wealth crowd out the reality and need to trust and know God? Do you think riches really bring happiness?

_____

CLOSING PRAYER

"God, I give you permission, and I ask you to help me understand more about what I read today...in Jesus' name I pray. Amen."

MY THOUGHTS:_____

_____

_____

QUESTIONS (John also invites you to email questions to john@findingtheanswerbook.com.):

_____

_____

_____

DAY 14

_____ (Initial & Date)

PRAYER

"God, here I am...I ask, through the power of Your Holy Spirit, that today, you show me who you are and that you love me...in Jesus' name I pray. Amen."

READING: Mark Chapter 10, Verses 32–52

THINK ABOUT:

- The concept of helping and serving others is something that is difficult in our world today because so many other things have our attention.
- Imagine how impossible the blind man felt trying to reach Jesus with hundreds, if not thousands. around him, BUT Jesus heard him and stopped to meet his request...Jesus is still the same today...
- Imagine if the beggar would not have believed and taken action—he would have missed his personal miracle.

_____

CLOSING PRAYER

"God, I give you permission, and I ask you to help me understand more about what I read today...in Jesus' name I pray. Amen."

MY THOUGHTS:_____

_____

_____

QUESTIONS (John also invites you to email questions to john@findingtheanswerbook.com.):

_____

_____

_____

DAY 15

_____(Initial & Date)

PRAYER

"God, here I am...I ask, through the power of Your Holy Spirit, that today, you show me who you are and that you love me...in Jesus' name I pray. Amen."

READING: Mark Chapter 11: Verses 1–33

THINK ABOUT:

- It's amazing to think that Jesus came back knowing he was going to face certain death...And he had the power to stop it but did not...
- Jesus showed his concern for average folks by his anger at the money changers...They were ripping off the people by cheating them on their change and exchange rates.
- Imagine knowing God so closely, that you know when you pray, he hears you and can answer your prayers...

_____

CLOSING PRAYER

"God, I give you permission, and I ask you to help me understand more about what I read today...in Jesus' name I pray. Amen."

MY THOUGHTS:_____

_____

_____

QUESTIONS (John also invites you to email questions to john@findingtheanswerbook.com.):

_____

To see a video about this topic from John Cale, open the camera on your phone, hold your phone over the QR code above, and click open on your browser.

DAY 16

_____(Initial & Date)

PRAYER

"God, here I am...I ask, through the power of Your Holy Spirit, that today, you show me who you are and that you love me...in Jesus' name I pray. Amen."

READING: Mark Chapter 12: Verses 1—17

THINK ABOUT:

- The tenants abused the very one who set them up and blessed their lives...They forgot what he had done...Has this happened to you?
- How often do we stop and think about God and the blessings we have in our lives? Someone always has it tougher than us...
- Jesus did not pick a "political" side...He urged people to honor their government, and in this case, that meant paying taxes...Ultimately, though, God deserves our highest allegiance.

_____

CLOSING PRAYER

"God, I give you permission, and I ask you to help me understand more about what I read today...in Jesus' name I pray. Amen."

MY THOUGHTS:_____

_____

_____

QUESTIONS (John also invites you to email questions to john@findingtheanswerbook.com.):

_____

_____

_____

DAY 17

_____(Initial & Date)

PRAYER

"God, here I am...I ask, through the power of your Holy Spirit, that today, you show me who you are and that you love me today...in Jesus' name I pray. Amen."

READING: Mark Chapter 12: Verses 18–44

THINK ABOUT:

- What are your thoughts about "Resurrection" from the dead? Jesus indicated there is a life after death in this passage.
- Do you feel religion is complicated? Is it just rules and perfection? Jesus says here there are really two rules...Love God and love your neighbor (people in your world) as yourself.
- Jesus is not impressed with how much we do or give...It is our heart and motive that matters.

_____

CLOSING PRAYER

"God, I give you permission, and I ask you to help me understand more about what I read today...in Jesus' name I pray. Amen."

MY THOUGHTS:_____

_____

_____

QUESTIONS (John also invites you to email questions to john@findingtheanswerbook.com.):

_____

_____

_____

DAY 18

_____(Initial & Date)

PRAYER

"God, here I am...I ask, through the power of your Holy Spirit, that today, you show me who you are and that you love me...in Jesus' name I pray. Amen."

READING: Mark Chapter 13: Verses 1–37

THINK ABOUT:

- Jesus answered his disciple's questions...He warns that signs will help us know the season of His return...like we can tell the change of seasons within a year.
- Jesus indicates He will return to get us...Do a search on "rapture" on Bible Gateway to learn more.
- Can you tell a "real" Bible teacher vs. a "false" one? You can ask God to let you know in your heart that what you are hearing is truth.

_____

CLOSING PRAYER

"God, I give you permission, and I ask you to help me understand more about what I read today...in Jesus' name I pray. Amen."

MY THOUGHTS:_____

_____

_____

QUESTIONS (John also invites you to email questions to john@findingtheanswerbook.com.):

_____

_____

_____

DAY 19

_____(Initial & Date)

PRAYER

"God, here I am...I ask, through the power of your Holy Spirit, that today, you show me who you are and that you love me...in Jesus' name I pray. Amen."

READING: Mark Chapter 14: Verses 1–26

THINK ABOUT:

- People judged the lady in the first part of this chapter for her act that was pure and motivated from her heart...Do you ever feel people misunderstand you and your true motives?
- Can you imagine the emotions Judas felt in betraying Jesus? He had walked with him for three years and seen the miracles...BUT money pulled him away, and satan used Judas' humanness.
- The Last Supper...Jesus knew He would be arrested and ultimately killed...This was his last time with His friends...Communion, as we know it, was instituted during The Last Supper.

_____

CLOSING PRAYER

"God, I give you permission, and I ask you to help me understand more about what I read today...in Jesus' name I pray. Amen."

MY THOUGHTS:_____

_____

_____

QUESTIONS (John also invites you to email questions to john@findingtheanswerbook.com.):

_____

_____

DAY 20   _____(Initial & Date)

PRAYER

"God, here I am...I ask, through the power of Your Holy Spirit, that today, you show me who you are and that you love me...in Jesus' name I pray. Amen."

READING: Mark Chapter 14: Verses 27–42

THINK ABOUT:

- Jesus knew Peter's human tendency to cave under pressure, and Jesus told Peter he would deny him three times that very night because of fear of harm to himself.
- Peter meant it when he thought he would not deny Jesus. Have you had times where your resolve was strong, but you failed? How did you feel and handle it?
- Jesus also shows his own human side as he considered the agony of the cross and he didn't cave under pressure. He knew it would be painful... Jesus had to reject using his power as God's Son that he could have used against mere humans to be obedient to his Father to die on the cross to pay the price for our sins.

_____

CLOSING PRAYER

"God, I give you permission, and I ask you to help me understand more about what I read today...in Jesus' name I pray. Amen."

MY THOUGHTS:_____

_____

_____

QUESTIONS (John also invites you to email questions to john@findingtheanswerbook.com.):

_____

# DAY 21
_____(Initial & Date)

PRAYER

"God, here I am...I ask, through the power of your Holy Spirit, that today, you show me who you are and that you love me...in Jesus' name I pray. Amen."

READING: Mark Chapter 14, Verses 43–72

THINK ABOUT:

- Jesus had the right to retaliate like we would, but he did not...Think about his commitment to die for us...
- Jesus was fully human and God...Imagine how he felt when everyone left him when he needed them most...Have you experienced this kind of betrayal?
- Imagine how Peter felt when he denied knowing Jesus just as Jesus predicted. The guilt of failing and letting his friend down was real. What times of failure and loneliness have you experienced?

_____

CLOSING PRAYER

"God, I give you permission, and I ask you to help me understand more about what I read today...in Jesus' name I pray. Amen."

MY THOUGHTS:_____

_____

_____

QUESTIONS (John also invites you to email questions to john@findingtheanswerbook.com.):

_____

_____

_____

# DAY 22
_____(Initial & Date)

PRAYER

"God, here I am...I ask through the power of your Holy Spirit, that today, you show me who you are and that you love me...in Jesus' name I pray. Amen."

READING: Mark Chapter 15, Verses 1–24

THINK ABOUT:

- Jesus' focus on his mission to die for our sins was so strong that he would not fall short of accomplishing it...Jesus willingly laid his life down for us.
- Imagine how Barabbas felt being released after he had committed crimes when Jesus was kept for doing nothing wrong. Jesus took Barabbas "penalty" just as Jesus takes the penalty for our sin when we believe in him and his power over death.
- The beating and abuse Jesus faced was exhausting...He fell under the cross he carried...Simon carried the cross for Jesus. Jesus faced this extreme suffering as a man, just as if it were you or I were enduring it. The pain and anguish were real.

_____

CLOSING PRAYER

"God, I give you permission, and I ask you to help me understand more about what I read today...in Jesus' name I pray. Amen."

MY THOUGHTS:_____

_____

_____

QUESTIONS (John also invites you to email questions to john@findingtheanswerbook.com.):

_____

_____

DAY 23

_____(Initial & Date)

PRAYER

"God, here I am...I ask, through the power of your Holy Spirit, that today, you show me who you are and that you love me...in Jesus' name I pray. Amen."

READING: Mark Chapter 15, Verses 25–47

THINK ABOUT:

- Jesus, an innocent man, allowed himself to selflessly be murdered on a cross because of his love for us. Think about this action for a moment...
- Jesus' response to the thief shows us that it is our belief and acceptance of him that changes us...The thief had no time to go apologize or do works...He simply accepted Jesus as Lord and wanted to be with him.
- The curtain in the temple was torn "top to bottom" signifying that mankind (we) now had direct access to God the Father through Jesus' death.

_____

CLOSING PRAYER

"God, I give you permission, and I ask you to help me understand more about what I read today...in Jesus' name I pray. Amen."

MY THOUGHTS:_____

_____

_____

QUESTIONS (John also invites you to email questions to john@findingtheanswerbook.com.):

_____

_____

_____

DAY 24

_____(Initial & Date)

PRAYER

"God, here I am...I ask, through the power of Your Holy Spirit, that today, you show me who you are and that you love me today...in Jesus' name I pray. Amen."

READING: Mark Chapter 16, Verses 1–13

THINK ABOUT:

- Jesus truly does defy death and nature as he rose from the dead on the third day.
- Imagine how the ladies felt seeing the robed man in white in the tomb and the stone was rolled away for them.
- Jesus appears to many people after his death confirming his Resurrection from the dead just as he said.

_____

CLOSING PRAYER

"God, I give you permission, and I ask you to help me understand more about what I read today...in Jesus' name I pray. Amen."

MY THOUGHTS: _____

_____

_____

QUESTIONS (John also invites you to email questions to john@findingtheanswerbook.com.):

_____

_____

_____

DAY 25

_____ (Initial & Date)

PRAYER

"God, here I am...I ask, through the power of your Holy Spirit, that today, you show me who you are and that you love me today...In Jesus' name I pray. Amen."

READING: Mark Chapter 16, Verses 14–20

THINK ABOUT:

- With his last words to his disciples, Jesus emphasized the importance of them spreading his message of love and forgiveness (referred to as the good news) by telling people everywhere.
- According to Jesus, to be saved and forgiven, we simply need to believe and be baptized...Doesn't this seem less complicated compared to all the confusion you might have heard about God?
- Imagine that Jesus' whole mission was to come here to die for us so we could be forgiven and adopted into his family. He did it all so that we could be acceptable to God the Father and have communication with him.

_____

CLOSING PRAYER

"God, I give you permission, and I ask you to help me understand more about what I read today...in Jesus' name I pray. Amen."

MY THOUGHTS:_____

_____

QUESTIONS (John also invites you to email questions to john@findingtheanswerbook.com.):

_____

To see a video about this topic from John Cale, open the camera on your phone, hold your phone over the QR code above, and click open on your browser.

OPTION 2
MEETING HIM

OPTION 2—MEETING HIM

It is awesome that you have chosen to come to this section. Arriving here does not prove anything or generate any benefit for anyone else BUT YOU. This whole book and the reflections you have experienced have been simply a vehicle to guide your attention and focus to a place and an invitation, which has existed for a long time...

So much could be written and outlined for you at this point, when you are, for the first time, having a discussion with God about your life and his reality. But I want to keep things simple and very to the point for you. Just like when you meet someone for the first time, you don't know all the things about their background, personality, etc...It is the same with God when you meet him. You simply have to make a decision to start the relationship, and as time passes, you can get to know him better and develop your relationship with him.

The challenge you may have faced up to this point is that you have had so many circumstances, disappointments, and noise in your life that have kept your attention distracted from hearing his call and realizing the invitation that he has prepared for you...The invitation has been there. I think you would agree that we have all had times in our lives when we have been so busy with other things that we missed an appointment or an event. After the fact, we felt horrible or embarrassed. THIS INVITATION IS NOT ONE YOU WANT TO IGNORE BECAUSE IT CAN REVOLUTIONIZE YOUR LIFE.

A SIMPLE PRAYER

God, I give you permission to speak to me and bring understanding to my mind as I read the following information. Help me to see the truth and to be open and honest...in Jesus' name I pray...Amen

SOME BASIC FACTS FOR YOUR CONSIDERATION BEFORE YOU MEET HIM:

1. In Genesis (The first book of the Bible), mankind disobeyed God and sin (a barrier of disobedience between man and God's relationship) entered the world. From this point forward, a separation existed between man and God because of this disobedience.

2. God began creating a pathway in history outlined throughout the Old Testament of the Bible to restore the ability for mankind to have a direct relationship with him. He created this pathway by orchestrating the sending of Jesus, his only Son, to Earth, to be born and ultimately to die, once and for all, for all mankind as a sacrifice for sin and disobedience. The birth of Jesus was written and predicted hundreds of years before Jesus was born. Jesus' birth was so significant that it split time as we know it into before his birth and after his birth. You may have heard these time frames referred to as B.C and A.D. By believing in Jesus and acknowledging that by his death our sins are forgiven, we can be acceptable to God because we know Jesus...Think of it as an exchange. When your lawyer represents you in court, he speaks on your behalf to the judge. Similarly, Jesus speaks on your behalf to his Father and says "He/She is with me." So the Father accepts us through Jesus.

3. You cannot earn His forgiveness or love. Think of your family or children...You love them even when they are unlovable at times...You can't be good enough, give enough, or go to church enough to get or earn a perfect God's love. Read the verse below:

Ephesians 2:8—9 (NIV)
> [8] For it is by grace you have been saved, through faith—and this is not from yourselves, it is the gift of God—
> [9] not by works, so that no one can boast.

When someone offers you a gift, do you ask "What do I owe you?" Of course not. You accept it and say thank you. This verse says your forgiveness is "the gift of God." It also says you can't earn forgiveness with your works. You must simply accept His forgiveness. He gives it to us because of his grace...What is grace? It is UNMERITED FAVOR, meaning that God is not treating us nor is He giving us the real punishment we deserve.

4. Jesus promised that if we are sincere and persistent in pursuing him, we will find him. Look at this verse, which records Jesus' words:

Matthew 7:7—8 (NIV)
> [7] Ask and it will be given to you; seek and you will find; knock and the door will be opened to you. [8] For everyone who asks receives; the one who seeks finds; and to the one who knocks, the door will be opened.

You have been following this verse without even knowing it...Your reading of this book and getting here has passed the "seek" and "knock" test. He promises that if you are diligent and sincere you will find him...So he is prepared and ready... Are you?

5. God is not about waiting around every corner to nail you for doing something wrong...He loves you. He does have guidelines and standards we need to follow which you will learn, and his Spirit can reveal as you get to know God—day in and day out. Look at what one of the most popular verses in the Bible says:

John 3:16—17 (NIV)
> [16] For God so loved the world that he gave his one and only Son, that whoever believes in him shall not perish but have eternal life. [17] For God did not send his Son into the world to condemn the world, but to save the world through him.

God wants to restore the relationship with us, which is what motivated him to send Jesus. Believing in Jesus and in his death, which pays the price for our sins, choosing to repent (making a turnaround in your life at the moment you decide), and developing your personal relationship with God daily is the secret to lasting change.

TO ACCEPT THE ANSWER AND TO RECEIVE HIS GIFT:

1. You have to acknowledge your belief that Jesus is the son of God and that He was born here on Earth and died on a cross to pay the price of your sins, once and for all, with his perfect and holy life.

2. You need to acknowledge that you are a sinner and separated from God in your natural state. We are all in this state before we ask for forgiveness.

3. You need to be genuine and realize that meeting with him and giving him permission to enter into your life is a decision at a point in time. From this point on, things begin to change, and the change occurs from inside out. As in any relationship, it will grow stronger over time as you spend time developing it.

YOUR INVITATION OF PRAYER TO GOD:

1 John 1:9 (NIV) says:
> [9] If we confess our sins, he is faithful and just and will forgive us our sins and purify us from all unrighteousness.

So, we have arrived at your opportunity to acknowledge the invitation that has been waiting...for you to provide permission for God to enter your life and bring peace and forgiveness...for you to find The Answer.

Please pray the following:

"God, I come before you, believing the things I have heard and read. I don't understand them all, but I do believe that Jesus is your Son and that he died on the cross to pay for my sins and was raised from the dead. I open my heart and life to you right now. I confess the sins from my life (If there is anything specific that comes to your mind, confess it to him) ...Things I cannot even remember, I ask you to forgive me. I invite you to enter my mind, my life, and change me. I choose to accept the gift of your forgiveness for me and make it mine.

I now thank you for answering my prayer, and I tell you that I accept your forgiveness. I thank you for speaking to me and leading me to this decision in Jesus' name I pray. Amen."

Welcome! You have just been adopted into God's family...very much like adoption here in our society. You have become part of his family, and you will be treated like one of the family.

WHERE DO I GO FROM HERE?

1 John 1:9 says
⁹ If we confess our sins, he is faithful and just and will forgive us our sins and purify us from all unrighteousness.

1. Please go to "The Challenge" section of this book and spend 25 minutes a day getting to know about him if you have not already done that.
2. John would love to hear about your experience. He invites you to email him by writing to john@findingtheanswerbook.com.
3. Be sensitive to slight changes that will likely occur in the days to come...a new sense of peace, joy, a different view...on life and the things around you. Literally think of it as looking through a different lens.
4. Call someone you know who has made this choice, who knows God and is someone you trust. Share with that person what has happened to you.
5. Find a local place to go to church and worship during the next available time that you can. This action is important so that you will be with folks who have experienced what you have and believe the same way you now do.
6. Consider shopping at Christianbook.com or visiting a local Christian Book store if there is one in your area. Review the materials, resources, and books that can help you continue on this new journey.
7. One book to consider is Lee Strobel's *The Case for Christ*, which is a story by a journalist who set out to prove God was a hoax and ultimately proved God's reality. The journalist then opened his life to God. *The Case for Christ* covers his journey and shares extensive facts that he uncovered.
8. Recommend *Finding The Answer* to your friends and family whose lives would indicate that they are still searching for The Answer.

ABOUT THE AUTHOR

John Cale considers himself a normal guy who has experienced loss, hurt, and happiness in life.

John grew up the son of Bodie Sr. and Stella Cale, an average blue-collar, hardworking, honest couple. John attended Mt. Carmel High School (a private academic boarding school) in Kentucky, where he received a solid life foundation and was cared for and specifically mentored by Verdon Higgins, the school's principle.

John went to college at several schools and completed his first degree. At the core, he always felt pulled into business, and he worked to help companies drive growth and revenue. Ultimately, John founded a tech company with two friends and changed the way banks look at and reach their consumers using the digital spectrum. His career also included a VP of sales position and working in healthcare.

He wrote this book not as someone who has figured it all out, but as someone who has made many mistakes and bad choices in life, some of which have hurt many people he loved. He has had to go back and ask for forgiveness.

Both his successes and his mistakes have led John to teach and lead others, a skill he also used as a teacher to junior high and high school students. as well as leading or serving on missions' trips to Russia, the Caribbean, New Mexico, Brazil, Israel, and Jordan.

John realized based on facts and experience that The Answer to life was there and available for him all along...but many times he ignored it. If he could go back, he would have listened to those who were older and wiser than he was, and he would have spent more time in prayer.

John speaks on life issues like finding your strengths, family matters, mentoring youth, assessing readiness for relationships, entrepreneurship, driving revenue, using data to find a pathway to growth in business, and other issues.

ABOUT THE ILLUSTRATOR

Bethany Migliore is a graphic artist with more than 20 years of experience. A graduate of Daemen College in Buffalo, New York, she now resides in Ohio with her husband and two children.

Findingtheanswerbook.com

John invites you to visit the ***FINDING THE ANSWER*** book website to:

- **Watch an Introductory Video**–Meet John, the man behind the words, along with his enthusiastic, hairy canine son "Jonsie." In this quick 2-minute video, John shares his overall thoughts about the book as well as a bit about his background.
- **Interact**–John is excited to hear about your thoughts and experience as you move through the book. He looks forward to learning about any changes in your life that you'd like to share with him. Simply click the link to email John.
- **Spread the Word about *FINDING THE ANSWER***–Easily introduce your family and friends to the book by giving them the URL, **findingtheanswerbook.com**. With this link, others can get to know John a bit, and they can explore reading ***Finding the Answer*** for themselves.
- **Schedule a Speaking Engagement with John**–If you'd like John to personally address your church or community, request that John come to speak to your group. He addresses a wide array of topics including forming life strategies, taking calculated risk, engaging in successful communication, fostering healthy family dynamics, and equipping leadership in your church, business, or community group. John welcomes bookings for a single speaking session or multiple sessions in the same visit.

NOTES

1. *LEXICO, Powered by Oxford, US Dictionary,* s.v. "answer," accessed July 26, 2022, https://www.lexico.com/en/definition/answer.

2. *Oxford Learner's Dictionary,* s.v. "relationship," accessed July 26, 2022, https://www.oxfordlearnersdictionaries.com/definition/american_english/relationship.

www.ingramcontent.com/pod-product-compliance
Lightning Source LLC
LaVergne TN
LVHW061257060426
835508LV00015B/1408